Beat Identity Theft

Reduce Your Risk and Fight Back!

Isabel Hogue

with J.R. Woodrum

This publication is intended to provide competent and reliable information regarding the subject matter. It is sold and offered with the understanding that the authors are not engaged in rendering any legal, financial, or other professional advice. Laws and practices vary from state to state. If legal or other expert assistance is required, please seek the services of a professional in your state. The authors specifically disclaim any liability that is incurred from the use of or application of the contents of this book.

Personal stories included in the book may be changed slightly to protect the privacy of the individuals involved. We have done our best to credit the source for stories we found online or in a published record.

Visit our website and blog *beatidentitytheftbook.com*

Please write a review on Amazon.com.

Quantity discounts are available. Send your request to

help@beatidentitytheftbook.com or call 765-323-8347

ISBN-13: 978-1490510477 (CreateSpace-Assigned)
ISBN-10: 1490510478

Contents

Change before you have to.

Jack Welch

Introduction

If you are concerned about identity theft, this book is for you.

It came about when, in our separate insurance and real estate practices, we heard stories about bad things happening to good people because of identity theft. We also saw situations where legal advice could have improved someone's life, but they didn't ask for help because attorneys are expensive.

We initially started looking for solutions to the problem of identity theft. Along our journey, we discovered that most identity theft protection plans on the market today give people a false sense of security. Identity theft cannot be prevented, yet the industry uses the word "prevention" to describe the plans. You can, and should, do some things to reduce your risk; but no system of "protection" is impenetrable, and no monitoring program is perfect.

As a result, most people are buying the wrong kind of identity theft protection service. They discover, too late, that they are on their own when it comes to unraveling the work of identity thieves and are at the mercy of the legal system when it comes to fighting back.

The crime of identity theft is growing. According to an estimate from the Federal Trade Commission (FTC), there are nine million victims a year. Some victims restore their accounts with little difficulty. Others must fight off creditors, endlessly prove that they are who they say they are, or even defend themselves against a criminal record.

In this book, you'll read a lot of stories that will help you understand your risk of identity theft. Some stories were told to us by people we know. To protect their privacy, we've done our best to conceal their identity.

Other stories we discovered through research, and we've done our best to credit their sources.

We're learning new stories every day. If you'd like to read more, visit beatidentitytheftbook.com/blog. We invite you to reply to a blog post and share your own story and tell others the most important things you learned from this book.

The reality of identity theft is that it's just a matter of time before you experience it. Yet most people wait until after an incident has occurred to find ways they could have saved time, money, and aggravation. Sometimes the reason is because the solutions were not in plain sight from the beginning.

This book presents solutions. Ignore them and you'll kick yourself when identity thieves strike. Take action and you'll be forever grateful that you did. It's kind of like buying a fire extinguisher. You need to get one before you need it because when you need it, *you need it*.

The solutions take the form of three concepts:

Concept #1 Learn the simple things you can start doing to reduce your risk. This includes being careful with your personal information, your passwords, and pin numbers; keeping a watchful eye on your accounts, benefits, and mail; and guarding what you say to other people.

Concept #2 Own an identity theft protection plan that offers a restoration service, including licensed investigators who will work on your behalf to resolve the damage.

Concept #3 Own a legal protection plan. Every identity theft incident is a legal event. The sooner you can get advice and counsel, the better off you'll be. Legal protection plans are revolutionizing the delivery of legal services in the United States by giving people access to the help they need without having to pay an attorney by the hour. The advantage of a legal protection plan is that it can help you in every area of your life, not just identity theft defense.

We live in a world of changing technology. To survive, you must change along with it. We strongly believe a necessary change is your willingness to embrace new business models and new ways of accessing the help and services you need. This book makes no representation on behalf of or any endorsement of any specific product or company. This book is intended to be a discussion of important risk management concepts only.

This book is about beating the crime of identity theft by introducing strategies and tactics that reduce your risk and enhance your ability to fight back.

The majority of victims do not know how their identifying information was compromised. The question these victims most commonly ask when they call the FTC's identity theft hotline is, "how could this have happened to me?" Our answer is that it could have arisen in a multitude of ways.

Betsy Broder

Assistant Director for the Division of Planning and Information of the Bureau of Consumer Protection, Federal Trade Commission

Chapter 1

What you ought to know

about identity theft

"Someone is trying to steal my identity!" Grandma said. "They're sending me threatening letters."

Threatening letters? Grandma's daughters looked through her mail. The threatening letters turned out to be direct mail solicitations for an identity theft protection product. In big, bold letters at the bottom of each letter were the words: YOU could be next!!!

Grandma was wrong about the threatening letters, but she was right about one thing: becoming a victim of identity theft is scary. Like many people, Grandma was afraid of identity theft. Perhaps you picked up this book because you're concerned – or skeptical – that you could be next.

If you haven't already been a victim of identity theft, you may be under the seduction of normalcy.

How are you being seduced?

The seduction of normalcy happens to you when you know, on the one hand, that something bad like identity theft could disrupt your life. On the other hand, nothing bad has actually happened to you. As a result, you feel safe and secure in going about your normal routine.

You may even be doing some smart things to protect yourself from identity theft. You shred papers before putting them in the trash. You trust your credit card company to call you and report an unusual charge. You pay cash at restaurants. You're on the Do Not Call Registry. You don't talk to telemarketers. You lock your car. You lock your home, and maybe you have a security system.

You feel like you've covered the most important bases. Deep down, you believe that if identity thieves strike, your bank will take care of it.

How can smart people become victims of identity theft?

The truth is none of us can completely crime-proof our lives. Many identity theft incidents involve information that came from data or files that are in someone else's possession. A theft can happen because employees are not properly trained to protect your information, because they are careless with it, or because they steal it. Smart people can become victims because computer technology has made it so easy for identity thieves to access your personal information and use it against you. Thieves grab your information either directly or by piecing it together from various sources.

You can't totally prevent identity theft from happening. The more aware you become about the many ways you are exposed to identity theft, the more you can do to reduce your risk of becoming a victim.

More important, your knowledge will help you take quick action to minimize the damage when identity thieves strike.

The damage identity thieves are doing to individuals, businesses, and government has prompted the creation of countless new non-profit organizations, government agencies, and a growing service industry for protection products. In 2012, there were 79 companies [1] offering identity theft protection services, but with mixed reviews from consumer advocacy groups.

How will this book empower you?

It was because of the mixed reviews we encountered that we began looking deeper into the subject of identity theft protection. We wanted to cut through the industry hype surrounding the plans and get to the truth. Getting to the truth was especially important because we sell identity theft and legal protection plans. Our reputations depend on selecting products that offer an honest value.

We are not attorneys so don't take this book as legal advice. It isn't. Rather, take this book as a tool that can help save you hours of time, thousands of dollars, and untold emotional stress. We've spent a lot of time researching all aspects of identity theft and simply want to share some of what we've learned with the hope of helping other people.

The more we learned about the subject, the more concerned we became about the misconceptions people have about identity theft, identity theft protection plans, and taking legal action after a crime has been committed.

Our conclusions may surprise you. They may not please some of the leaders in the identity theft protection services industry. That's okay. The field of identity theft protection is still relatively new, with plenty of competition. We believe that our small contribution will add to the continuing development of industry best practices. Openly sharing lessons learned is how businesses and consumers figure out what works best.

This book will give you some information on what you can do to manage the risk of identity theft so you can live worry-free and stay focused on your life and work. No single source about identity theft can provide all of the answers. We're all still learning about this crime and the methods criminals are using to commit it.

Finally, this book will give you some specific recommendations of plans to put in place that will save you money and time and make your life a heck of a lot easier. That's empowering.

Why is protecting your privacy important?

Identity theft is a crime that puts at risk your privacy, your finances, your family, your independence, and possibly your future. You can't afford to ignore it.

Many people understand why protecting their finances, family, independence, and future are important. But many do not understand why privacy is important. When you bring up the subject, they'll laugh and say, "I don't have anything to hide!"

Privacy is not about hiding something. It's about protecting something. The Bill of Rights does not specifically spell out the privacy rights of a United States citizen. As a consequence, your rights are open to interpretation by the courts and can change over time. Your right to privacy is important in protecting you against crimes such as fraud, scams, and identity theft. It's also important in protecting you against government intrusion and tyranny. Protecting your privacy is an important part of understanding the front end of identity theft.

What can you do on the front end?

The front end of identity theft concerns attitudes and behaviors you can control that can give you the ability to make yourself a less attractive target for thieves. It also concerns the many things you cannot control that give an identity thief access to your personal information. The harsh reality is this: on the front end of identity theft, total prevention is impossible. Nevertheless, taking steps to deter or prevent identity theft is the responsible thing to do.

How do the bells and whistles help you?

You'll find that most of the emphasis for consumers about identity theft is on the front end of the problem. There's plenty of advice about what to do and what not to do, and some of it gets downright complicated and overwhelming. Your challenge is to simplify the advice into steps you will actually take that minimize your risk of becoming a victim.

Detection, monitoring, and alerts are the other areas of emphasis for consumers on the front end. While they are important, detection, monitoring, and alerts let you know that something has already happened. They are not preventive and may give you a false sense of security.

Despite the feeling of being overwhelmed and the limitations of consumer protections, anything you can incorporate into your daily routine that will make you a tougher target of opportunity is worth doing.

What can you do on the back end?

The back end of identity theft involves the damage control you must initiate in order to restore your life to normal after your identity has been stolen, used, and abused.

As with so many things in life, the back end is where you'll experience the most pain. An identity theft incident will cost you in terms of time, productivity, money, and emotional stress. How much it will cost depends on how quickly you detect the crime and the type of identity theft. Regardless of the cost, victims of identity theft experience emotional trauma, the same as do victims of other crimes.

What's the worst part of identity theft?

The worst part is that you are on your own when it comes to cleaning up the mess other people have made of your life.

It's up to you to prove your innocence, to file the police report, and to contact every institution, government agency, utility, business, credit bureaus, and anyone else who may be involved. The burden of proof is on you.

"Victims of identity theft need a support team to get through complex cases," says Linda Forshey, founder of the nonprofit Identity Theft Resource Center. An identity theft victim is always better off when there is someone to explain and champion their consumer rights. If the situation is serious enough, you may need to hire an attorney.

Getting legal help can be scary. First of all, an attorney's high hourly rate is a financial challenge that prompts people to try to solve problems on their own. Second, finding an experienced, competent attorney that you can really trust can be intimidating under the best of circumstances.

When you must find an attorney to help manage a legal crisis, the selection process can be overwhelming. Most people are not familiar with the language of lawyers or navigating the unfamiliar territory of our legal system. They will invest more time shopping for a car they'll drive for three years than they will spend looking for an attorney who can change the course of their life. "By the time people come to see me," an attorney told us, "it's all remedial."

What's a better way to manage the risk?

That's why we've come to the realization that having an identity theft restoration service is as necessary as having home or auto insurance.

Don't make the mistake of thinking all identity theft protection plans offer equal protection. If you have a plan or a rider on your homeowner's policy, you'd better get it out and read the fine print.

Many identity theft protection plans offer monitoring and counseling services to help you on the front end. Other plans or policy riders only reimburse you for time and out of pocket expenses you incur when trying to straighten out the mess. Those are all valuable features, but the game-changer is having a restoration service that will do the work for you on the back end.

Few of us have the experience to efficiently do what it takes to restore the damage identity thieves have done. Where we desperately need the help is in knowing what to do and how to do it.

An identity theft protection plan with a restoration service, in combination with a legal protection plan, gives you immediate access to experienced experts who can guide, represent, and work for you until the restoration of your identity is complete.

In fact, taking advantage of services like these gives you and your family access to expert advice early in the game so that you make better decisions and minimize the stress.

It's the kind of help that could be mighty welcome someday because, regardless of whether or not you've been a victim, YOU could be next!!!

Review

- Beware of the "seduction of normalcy."

- No one is too smart to become a victim.

- Total prevention of identity theft is impossible.

- When you are an identity theft victim, the damage control is up to you.

- You need support because dealing with identity theft is stressful.

- Get an identity theft protection plan that includes restoration services.

Criminals obtain the vital numbers using various tactics, often by bribing office workers with access to personnel files inside companies, as well as large public institutions such as hospitals and schools, according to prosecutors.

"Florida hit by 'tsunami' of tax identity fraud"

David Adams

Chapter 2

Who wants your identifiable information?

An Oregon man walked into his bank to investigate why more than $700 in checks had been written on his account. While he was there, the identity thief came in to the bank and tried to cash one more check. [2]

An Indiana woman went to her bank to investigate why her account had been drained. While she was there, the identity thief from Poland called the bank on the phone and tried to withdraw more money. [3]

In both cases, the identity theft was detected early, easily proven, and stopped.

These stories teach us two things. First, identity thieves can reach you from where you live or from anywhere in the world. Second, these two victims were fortunate in that they caught the crime early.

How did this modern crime epidemic start?

These days, almost everyone knows a story about fraudulent use of debit cards, credit cards, and checks. Perhaps that's one reason why people think banking and credit card fraud is all there is to identity theft. But the problem is bigger than that.

Identity theft involves intentionally transferring or using somebody else's means of identification to do something that breaks a federal, state, or local law. [4] In other words, identity theft is about the misuse of your mailing address, your driver's license, your Social Security number, your health insurance, and more.

In real life, the lines between identity theft, fraud, and scams are blurred. Many of the activities that people think of as "identity theft" are better classified as fraudulent transactions. Some people are sticklers for using the correct terms. Sometimes it's important; sometimes it's not.

When identity theft happens to you, we doubt you'll become obsessed with correcting everyone who calls it by the wrong name. You'll be focused on getting your money and restoring your own good name.

Identity theft and identity fraud are not new crimes. The crime wave we are experiencing today is partly due to the rise of electronic technology and the internet.

Starting around 1995, millions of people started using cellular phones, conducting electronic financial transactions, and using home computers connected to the internet. Few of us realized in the beginning how radically these conveniences would expose us to criminal activity.

Identity theft activity increased so rapidly that by 1998, law enforcement agencies, the U.S. Congress, the FTC, and other government agencies were overwhelmed with trying to help the victims and prevent the crime.

Today we're a lot smarter about preventing identity theft, but the thieves are a lot smarter too. As soon as we begin to feel secure in one area, we learn how they're exploiting our personal information in some other way. It's unsettling to realize that your sense of normalcy is often a mile wide and an inch deep.

Who is trying to steal your identity?

Identity thieves can be anyone from an isolated individual to someone connected to a domestic or international organized crime network.

The problem of criminal networks is world-wide in scope. According to a report issued by the President's Identity Theft Task Force 2007, the term "criminal networks" includes "motorcycle clubs, terrorist groups, street gangs, and organized criminal enterprises." [5] A network can be as few as two individuals working together to commit identity theft.

There are approximately 10,000 identity theft rings operating in the U.S., according to consumer risk management consulting firm ID Analytics, and the areas with the highest numbers of fraud rings are Tampa, Florida, Washington D.C., Greenville,

Mississippi, Macon, Georgia, Montgomery, Alabama, and Detroit, Michigan. Electronic technology and internet access enables them to find and use your personally identifiable information no matter where you live. [6] Your personally identifiable information (PII) includes any information that could be used, either alone or in combination with other information, to identify, contact, or locate you.

Identity thieves can be individuals operating alone. Some individuals may simply take advantage of an opportunity. For example, an identity thief could be an acquaintance, a friend, a neighbor, an employee, or a member of your own family, who has access to your personal information or identification. Your children are especially vulnerable to identity theft because the use of a child's Social Security number can go undetected for years.

Identity theft is a way that someone, such as an ex-boyfriend, girlfriend, or spouse can make your life miserable. Sometimes it's difficult to understand what motivates people to commit the crime.

One of our friends – Bonnie – told us how her own mother submitted credit card applications that came in the mail in Bonnie's name. When a card was issued, Bonnie's mom maxed out the spending limit. Bonnie was thousands of dollars in debt by the time she discovered what her mother had done. When Bonnie confronted her mom, she was without remorse. Bonnie's mom said it was her way of getting some financial benefit, which she believed her daughter owed to her.

Contrast Bonnie's experience with that of the Oregon man and the Indiana woman who discovered fraudulent bank transactions. Bonnie's story shows how easy it is for someone to commit identity theft and how painful the aftermath can be.

Why do thieves want your identity?

"Nobody would want to steal *my* identity. I don't have any money! They can *have* my identity!"

We've heard many people say things like that, and chuckle at the thought of having their identity stolen. These people don't know what they don't know!

Others mistakenly believe that identity theft is only about credit cards, debit cards, and bank accounts. In 2012, the FTC reported that only 17% of identity theft events were related to credit card and banking fraud. [7] While identity theft may result in financial loss, it's clear that thieves are often after more than just your money.

They're after your good name, your mother's maiden name, your home address, your driver's license, your health insurance, your Social Security number, and, really, whatever identifiable information they can get their hands on so that they can use the information to either commit or cover up other crimes.

How are they getting your information?

Theft of your "means of identification" can happen to you anywhere, anytime, and by anybody. Identity thieves can even deceive you into voluntarily giving them your information.

Thieves can pick up your personal information by:

- stealing your mail or breaking into your home,
- picking up something from your space at work or school,
- stealing from records stored at a business, organization, or government facility,
- using a cell phone to photograph your credit card or other identification, and
- scanning or "skimming" your information from your credit or debit card.

Data Breach

Most people think "hacker" when they hear the word *data breach*, but a data breach occurs any time that unauthorized personnel access your personally identifiable information or personal health information. This access could happen intentionally or by accident. The majority of data breaches occur because of employee negligence, criminal employees, or malicious computer attack. The bottom line is that your personally identifiable information is stored by other people. You cannot control who has access to it or where it might end up after a data breach.

It follows naturally that victims of data breach are more likely to become victims of identity theft. "The most common types of identity information leaked in deliberate data breaches was names, addresses, and credit card numbers; accounting for one-third of the identities breached in 2011," says a Symantec report. While computer hackers may be able to grab more data at a time, physical theft is still "the greatest source of data breaches last year according to the Norton Cybercrime Index data." Incidents of politically motivated data breaches are on the rise. [8]

In an intentional data breach, unscrupulous employees or computer hackers take your information, such as your Social Security number, and either use it themselves to commit fraudulent activity or sell it to others. This is why many victims of identity theft have no idea how the thieves got their information. Personally identifiable information is sold on hidden "black market" web pages where you can shop for illegal and stolen information. We recommend that you don't try looking for these web pages, unless you want to find out what it feels like to have a S.W.A.T. team invade your home.

The following story illustrates how quickly a data breach can lead to identity theft. In 2012, "approximately 3.8 million Social Security numbers, 387,000 credit and debit card numbers and 657,000 business tax filings were exposed in a recent security breach at the [South Carolina] Department of Revenue." [9] The breach was traced to an international hacker. Within days of the breach, Tina and Wade Mather's business bank account was "hacked and drained out of 4-thousand dollars [*sic*]. The only place they had that information [their business account] stored online was on the State Revenue Department's server." [10]

An unintentional data breach may occur because of a computer programming error. It also may occur when a computer, cell phone, or briefcase containing personally identifiable information is lost or stolen. It's a data breach when a letter, document, or email containing personally identifiable information is delivered to the wrong person. Regardless of the cause, every data breach that includes your information exposes you to identity theft.

The high probability and impact of data breach.

Large businesses, organizations, government, schools, and hospitals are targets for identity thieves. According to statistics released by the Open Security Foundation and DataLossDB, incidents of reported data loss by category are: business 52%, government 18%, medical 16%, and education 14%. [11] Medical facilities and schools are choice targets because they are easier to attack than financial institutions.

Most people don't know it, but schools and hospitals can use student and patient information to send targeted marketing and advertisements. [12] [13] [14] This practice gives vendors limited access to a database. While institutional administrators assure us that no academic or clinical information linked to an individual is shared with vendors or researchers, who's to say what can happen in the future?

An article in *The Tampa Tribune* states that "A national survey released in December [2012] found 94 percent of hospitals had suffered data breaches in the preceding two years." [15] The article lists common ways that identity thieves target medical records:

- photographing a doctor's office patient sign-in sheet that contains personal information
- retrieving records discarded in trash containers
- hacking into electronic databases
- employees stealing the data

Schools and colleges depend on electronic records and teaching materials. Students have computers and other devices that connect to the school network. This makes it easy for tech-savvy students to hack into the system. In Ketchikan, Alaska, a group of middle school students directed a phishing attack at their teachers. A phishing attack is sending a phony but official looking email that tricks the receiver into revealing a user name and password. The students were logged in to the network administrator account and remotely controlling more than 300 computers in the school system before they were caught. [16]

In the United States, medical facilities, schools, businesses, organizations, and governments have a legal responsibility to protect your information. They must disclose any use they make of it and report a data breach. The reporting requirement is particularly important if the revealing of your information could result in a violation of your privacy or cause harm or embarrassment. There is no single Federal law that requires businesses and organizations to notify you if a data breach occurs, but most states have enacted legislation that defines the circumstances and time requirements that require data breach notification. It's a good idea to get legal advice any time your identity has been stolen, but especially when the incident is the result of a data breach.

Break-ins

It used to be that when a home or business was burglarized, the thieves took *things* of value, such as computers, tools, TVs, jewelry, and cash. Now they are after personal information, blank checks, and other financial information.

A university student was arrested in Indiana for breaking into the office of an apartment complex. The student stole personal information from the files of tenants and used it to obtain loans and credit cards.

The student learned his methods from his brother and other relatives. A newspaper report states that "they used disposable cell phones and addresses for burned or abandoned homes to try to avoid getting caught." [17]

The student was committing a form of identity theft known as new account fraud. Reviewing your credit report periodically will help alert you to new accounts that have been opened in your name.

Your mail box

Identity thieves don't have to break in to your home
or business to steal your information. In Medford,
Oregon, up to 20 suspects were rounded up for stealing
from residential mail boxes. Up to 800 mail boxes were
involved, and thieves "stole mail, forged checks and got
illegal debit and credit cards. Besides mailboxes, they
broke into cars to get victims' information." Some
victims lost thousands of dollars. [18]

Thieves can use your personally identifiable
information to get almost anything they want—things
like housing, utilities, rental furniture, or cars—without
having to worry about paying the bills.

Isn't anybody safe?

In March 2013, the major credit reporting agencies
were hacked and the credit reports of several famous
people, including First Lady Michelle Obama, were
accessed and posted online.

The credit reporting company TransUnion said the
hackers "used 'considerable amounts' of personal

information including social-security numbers [*sic*] to impersonate victims and access their credit history." [19]

Almost all transactions are now electronic. Government benefits are issued electronically. Everyone now is required to have a Social Security number, including newborn children. Tax returns are filed electronically, and refunds are direct deposited. In some states, people even vote electronically. (And just so you know, it is illegal to vote under someone else's name. A Cincinnati grandmother was arrested in 2013 for submitting absentee ballots under the names of several of her family members.) [20]

In so many ways, bigger business and bigger government have opened bigger opportunities for identity theft. Nobody is safe from the threat. We have evolved into a society where opportunities for identity theft are easy and illicit profits are made quickly.

Where is the identity theft trend heading?

There are people out there right now looking for ways to steal your name, Social Security number, and whatever else they can grab.

By using your personal information, other people can hook up utilities, obtain medical treatment, file fraudulent medical claims, apply for government benefits, get jobs, claim your income tax refund, and steal elections.

Computers, mobile devices, and electronic transactions make it easier than ever for thieves to exploit you. Smartphone users, for example, are 33% more likely than others to become victims of identity fraud. [21] That number will only increase as more and more people switch to Smartphones and begin using mobile payment devices. This is because a Smartphone is a miniature computer that is easily lost or stolen. Nearly 62% of Smartphone users don't use a password to protect their phones. [22] Smartphone users are more likely than regular computer users to download apps or open email that contains malware or viruses.

The across-the-board trend is that as we get ahead of identity thieves in one area, they begin exploiting opportunities in another. This trend will not reverse.

Will you be next?

You can't prevent identity theft from happening because you can't control all of the variables. Your information is out of your hands.

In this environment of widespread criminal identity theft, your biggest weakness is your own sense of safety and invincibility. It's what holds you back from taking defensive action. It's kind of like the outlook of the Thanksgiving turkey. He had no cause to question his sense of safety, security, and trust in his friend the farmer, says author Nassim Taleb. But on the day before Thanksgiving, the turkey found out that his past experience was not a good predictor of what could happen to him in the future. [23]

Just because you never have been a victim of identity theft does not mean that you never will become one. In fact, you COULD be next!!!

How will you respond to identity theft?

Both of the stories about banking identity fraud at the beginning of this chapter had a good ending for the victims. The man in Oregon and the woman in Indiana got the bank fraud stopped because they were lucky that the thieves were obvious and because *the victims took quick action.*

These stories have an important lesson for you. Identity theft is a crime where it's up to you - the victim - to defend yourself, to prove that a crime took place, and to initiate corrective action.

When you become a victim of identity theft, fraud, or a scam, no matter how embarrassed or humiliated you feel, you can't hide or ignore the problem if you want to get on with your life.

How could an identity theft event challenge your sense of security, personal control, reputation, and peace of mind? Depending on the scope of the event, the challenge could be significant because it's up to you to confront the situation. It's up to you to do whatever it takes for as long as it takes. It's up to you to know and to defend your rights. It's up to you take time out to clean up the mess an offender has made of your life.

After an identity theft event, your life will never be quite the same as it was before. You'll be more vigilant and more careful. You may struggle with anger and have a hard time emotionally letting go of what happened.

What choice do you have?

What we are suggesting is that you can choose right now to face the truth about your exposure to identity theft. Don't wait until after the horse has been stolen to lock the barn door. Choose to make some changes in your attitude and behavior that will help reduce your risk of becoming the next victim.

Review

- Identity theft is a modern crime epidemic.

- Identity thieves can be connected to international or domestic crime networks, they can be individuals tempted by an opportunity, or they can be people you know— even family members.

- Identity thieves want YOUR personal information.

- You have no control over hackers and data thieves.

- When you are a victim, it's up to you to repair the damage and to know and defend your rights.

- You can choose to face the threat and take precautions.

Relying on the government to protect your privacy is like asking a peeping tom to install your window blinds.

John Perry Barlow

co-founder of an international non-profit digital rights group

Chapter 3

Do you have a false sense of security?

Simon Bunce of Hampshire, England lost his job, his reputation, and nearly lost his family after his stolen credit card was used to pay for child pornography.

In a 2004 operation, British law enforcement arrested 7,272 credit card holders whose numbers were on record with a U.S. company that handled transactions for pornographic websites. The transaction record alone was the basis for charging Mr. Bunce with possession of child pornography. He was innocent of the crime, and his wife believed in him, yet when his employer learned that he had been arrested, Mr. Bunce was fired from his job. He was cut off by his father and other relatives when they learned the nature of the charges. It was up to Simon Bunce to clear his name. [24]

Mr. Bunce's story demonstrates how becoming an identity theft victim can be a stressful event that leaves emotional scars. It took Mr. Bunce months to clear his name of the charges. He finally was able to get another, but less paying, job. However, his family relationships will never be the same. "I've forgiven them," said Mr. Bunce. "There's no point in bearing a grudge."

His story also shows how the damage from identity theft can reach far beyond your credit card and bank account. Regardless of whether your financial institution helps you resolve a minor incident quickly or your life becomes a nightmare, every identity theft victim is a crime victim. As a crime victim, you must know and protect your legal rights. To do that effectively, you may need the help of an attorney.

What are other ways your identity is at risk?

It's shocking to see the forms identity theft can take and the hardships the victims suffer. There's no way that, in one book, we can cover every aspect or angle of identity theft. That's why it's important to stay alert to the threats and be open to new ways to manage the risk.

As part of our research, we set a Google Alert to monitor new internet content for the term "identity theft." We encourage you to keep up to date by setting your own Google alert. Every day, one or two monitoring reports with eight or ten news items will arrive in your email in-box. Every day, you'll learn a new twist to this evolving criminal threat to your personal and financial well-being.

In this book, we'll look at five common categories of identity theft in. You'll see how your risk of identity theft goes far beyond banking and credit card fraud. In the back of this book, we've listed more ways your identity can be stolen.

Your credit card and bank account

Credit card fraud and bank fraud together account for only 25% of the financial identity thefts reported to the FTC. [25] That's only one-fourth of the problem.

Generally speaking, the thieves either access your existing credit card or bank account, or open new accounts in your name.

Check your existing account activity regularly, whether you receive a monthly statement or manage your account online. Avoid using debit cards. At least with a credit card, you can dispute the transaction and delay payment. With a debit card, the money is gone. You may or may not get it back.

It's also a good idea to stop writing checks. Identity thieves can use information from your check to access your existing bank account. The treasurer of a church told us that identity thieves from Nicargua somehow obtained a copy of a check written on the church account. The thieves were able to withdraw thousands of dollars from the church bank account. Electronic transactions are more secure. Written checks pass through many hands and can be copied or stolen.

To detect new account fraud, check your credit report and record of past addresses. You can do this by using the free annual credit reporting service created by the three nationwide consumer credit reporting companies. To use the service, either go to the website annualcreditreport.com or call 1-877-322-8228. This service offers you a free credit report once every 12 months from each of the consumer credit reporting companies: Equifax, Experian, and TransUnion.

Evidence of new account fraud is receiving collection notices or bills for accounts you don't recognize. Be sure to investigate financial activity that doesn't make sense, such as receiving collection notices you don't recognize or being turned down for insurance or a loan.

Your character and criminal record

An identity theft ring operating in several states obtained personal information by purse snatching, pick pocketing, mail theft, and recruiting office workers. The thieves then scanned the stolen driver's licenses and military IDs to create duplicate, false IDs. [26]

A woman who worked as a caregiver lost her job over identity theft. While the caregiver was at the public library, a thief picked her wallet from her purse. Later that day, the thief was arrested for shoplifting. The thief showed the police the caregiver's driver's license. As amazing as it seems, the police did not realize that the thief presented a stolen ID.

When the caregiver's employer saw the police report, the agency had no choice but to terminate the caregiver's employment. It was up to the caregiver to prove her innocence, and until she could clear her name, it was her word against the evidence of her own ID.

One of the biggest mistakes people make is leaving a purse or wallet in their car. Don't leave your purse of wallet unattended. Never place your purse in a grocery cart while you shop.

Thieves don't have to take your wallet. They only need to remove your ID, credit card, or tear out a check. In addition, the thief may pose as a Good

Samaritan and return your wallet or purse to you. You may feel grateful to find everything intact. The thief, however, could have copied your identification and credit cards before returning them.

It can be a long time before you discover what has happened; but by then, the thieves will have done a lot of damage using your identity. If the identity thieves have given your personally identifiable information while being arrested, you may now have a criminal record, a warrant for your arrest, or other related problems. You'll have to get help from law enforcement or the courts in order to clear your name. Better hire a lawyer, too.

Your Social Security number

Do not carry your Social Security card in your purse or wallet. Keep the card at home in a safe place.

You're probably aware that your Social Security number can be used by another person to obtain employment or to receive government benefits. However, you may not know how to monitor your earnings. You can check your Social Security benefits and monitor your earnings online by creating an account at socialsecurity.gov. It's a good idea to review your earnings at least once a year. The sooner you can find and correct a problem, the better off you'll be.

A lady named Mary Jones found out the hard way when her bank gave her Social Security number and account information to another customer who also was named Mary Jones. The other Mary Jones was a Bad Mary Jones, who opened credit card accounts in Good Mary's name, ran up the charges, and never paid the bills.

Bad Mary's fraudulent financial activities created such a mess that Good Mary finally had to request a new Social Security number. But that created more problems, because now Good Mary has to continually prove that her new Social Security number is valid.

Good Mary told us, "It's been ten years since the first incident, but to this day I still receive an occasional collection notice. They never give up." [27]

Your child's Social Security number

Children are more likely than adults to be victims of identity theft. A report issued by the Identity Theft Resource Center showed that the Social Security numbers of children under age 5 are prime targets for identity thieves.

This is because the use of a child's Social Security number will go undetected for many years. Many times, a family member will use the child's number to obtain loans or services. Unless the child's entire identity is used, the transactions may not show up on a credit report. It isn't until the child reaches the age when he or she begins seeking employment or student loans that the damage is discovered.

Monitoring the use of your child's Social Security number presents special challenges. It is against the law for you to create an online account for your child at the Social Security Administration's website ssa.gov so that you can monitor your child's Social Security account. Your child cannot set up his own account if he is under age 18. You will have to contact the Social Security

Administration directly if you think your child's number has been compromised. You will need documentation that proves your custody, relationship, and responsibility for your child.

Attempting to monitor your child's credit report can work against you. The Identity Theft Resource Center warns that checking a child's credit report too frequently can mask any activity that is coming from identity thieves. A child should not have a credit report. Your credit inquires will create a pattern of consumer activity. [28]

Nevertheless, you should be alert for warning signs, such as if your child receives a data breach notice from his or her school, a tax notice from the IRS, collection notices or he is turned down for insurance or a loan. The FTC's Consumer Information website consumer.ftc.gov is a reliable source of up-to-date information regarding what you can do as a parent to protect your child's Social Security number. This information can change as the laws change.

Your Medicare ID number

The ID number on your Medicare card is a Social Security number. It's probably your own Social Security number; but depending upon how you are eligible for the Medicare benefit, it could be the Social Security of a spouse or other qualifying individual.

Do not carry your Medicare card in your purse or wallet. It isn't necessary and it puts you at risk for identity theft.

Carry your Medicare card only when you visit a medical provider. They probably will photocopy the card, so you shouldn't need to show it every time you visit. Except when you are receiving medical services, leave the card at home in a safe place.

Not only does carrying your Medicare card put your Social Security number at risk, it exposes you to medical identity theft as well.

Your medical identity

When someone uses your identity to receive medical services or to produce fraudulent billing, it's medical identity theft.

A man used his credit card to pay for a prescription at a local pharmacy. A few days later, a charge appeared on his card from a pharmacy in the same chain but in another state.

The roommate of a young man we'll call Jim used Jim's ID to receive medical treatment in another state. Jim discovered the identity theft when he began receiving the bills. Jim had to prove that he was not the person who received the medical services.

While the financial aspects of medical identity theft are more readily detected, the changes to your medical record may not be discovered until a wrong treatment is prescribed and physical harm is done. It's practically impossible to monitor your medical records. That's why it's important to ask questions about what's on your record any time you receive medical treatment. Never assume that your medical record is without errors. This is especially important if your medical provider uses electronic records. Be alert to anything that doesn't seem right or make sense.

Even physicians are vulnerable to medical identity theft. International crime rings have been known to use the credentials of a physician to file fraudulent Medicare claims. [29]

According to an AARP study, stolen health insurance cards are being sold on the black market for $500 to $600. You may feel safe because your card is still in your wallet, but someone has access to a copy that is on file at a hospital or doctor's office. Don't kid yourself. You know they do.

Medical and dental practices are easy targets for identity theft. Your medical records are not safe. A study by the Ponemon Institute found that 94% of the healthcare organizations surveyed have experienced data breaches that exposed patient records. [30] In the spring of 2013, several individuals were arrested for stealing hundreds of medical records from Shands Jacksonville Medical Center, a University of Florida hospital. The thieves were using the information to file fraudulent income tax returns. [31]

Medical billing is so confusing that many people are unable to catch errors. If they see a problem, people are more likely to pass it off as a mistake, rather than suspect identity theft.

Another clue that you are a victim of medical identity theft is if you are declined for an insurance policy for medical conditions that you don't have.

Medical identity theft is now the fastest growing type of identity theft; and unlike in the banking and credit industries, there are almost no monitoring or anti-fraud procedures in place to protect you. Usually, it's first discovered when you begin receiving bills or collection notices from medical providers.

Watch for medical claims you don't recognize on your insurance explanation of benefits. If you are in doubt, call the provider or your insurance company.

Your income tax returns

Identity thieves need only your name and Social Security number to file a fraudulent electronic tax return. The thieves simply make up information about your address and W-2. They claim refunds for amounts under $3,000 and have the funds sent to a debit card account. In 2013, incidents of income tax return fraud grew exponentially. [32]

As with medical identity theft, your options for preventing tax fraud are limited at best. You will discover that you've been a victim when you file your income tax returns and receive notice that a return for that year has already been filed under your Social Security number. If you had a refund coming, you will not receive it until after the IRS has resolved the case. That could take months.

Have you got it covered?

Identity theft can damage your reputation. It can give you a criminal record and mess up your medical record, income tax returns, and Social Security record.

Yet a recent survey found that nearly 60% of Americans don't believe that identity theft is a serious problem. [33]

Even after reading about some of the more common areas of identity theft, and the fact that you cannot prevent it from happening, you may be the reader who still feels like you've got it covered because your bank or credit card company will "take care of it." Or because your brother-in-law is a lawyer (who works for free).

Review

- Monitor the news to keep up to date.
- Credit card fraud and bank fraud together account for only 25% of financial identity theft.
- Don't carry <u>any</u> card in your purse or wallet unless it's <u>absolutely necessary</u>.
- Don't use debit cards.
- Guard your personally identifiable information.

- Monitor your Social Security benefits and earnings online at socialsecurity.gov.

- Guard your child's Social Security number.

- Review medical claim summary notices for items you don't recognize.

- Report unusual tax notices from the IRS.

- Investigate financial activity that you don't recognize or that doesn't make sense.

Bonus Section

Famous last words:

- I think it's trying to communicate.

- I don't need to go to the hospital.

- I know what I'm doing.

- We've got them outnumbered.

- They'll never find it in here!

- I know a shortcut.

- I've got it covered . . ..

Despite the efforts of security professionals, information everywhere remains vulnerable and will continue to be seen as a ripe target by attackers with social engineering skills, until the weakest link in the security chain, the human link, has been strengthened.

The Art of Deception

Kevin Mitnick

Chapter 4

Deception techniques that will trip you up

Our friend Janet told us about the time her mother-in-law received a phone call from an identity thief. Janet was in the room when Mom answered the phone It was obvious from her body language that something was wrong.

"Put it on speaker phone," said Janet.

Mom turned on the speaker and Janet heard a woman's voice speaking English with a foreign accent. *"We have information that sixty-four computers in your area are being hacked right now. They are hacking into your computer as we speak! We are monitoring the situation. Please, go to your computer right now."*

"Tell her you're there," Janet said.

"I'm there," said Mom.

"Now tell me, what do you see?"

Mom, who is in her 80s and uncomfortable with computers, hesitated, then hung up the phone.

Janet was amazed at how well-trained the thief sounded, with a voice that was urgent, authoritative, and compelling.

Later Janet told this story to a friend, who said, "Oh my gosh! They called my mom, too. She actually went to her computer and was ready to give her credit card number when she felt like something was wrong and hung up."

Before this incident, Janet couldn't understand how anyone could be led into giving out their personal information over the phone to a stranger. Now she knows it can happen very easily.

What is social engineering?

Security experts use the term "social engineering" to describe the use of the psychological techniques of gaining trust or manipulation for the purpose of gathering information or gaining compliance. Social engineers use artful confidence tricks and deception techniques because they know that the strongest, most complex security systems man can create may be defeated with the help of a willing, compliant human being.

The psychological techniques work because most people are trusting of others, especially when that person is nice, seems knowledgeable, or is insistent.

What is the best defense?

One defense against social engineering is sharing stories and experiences. Talking with other people about what you've read, heard, and experienced helps raise your awareness level.

Our friend Janet reported six months later that her mother-in-law is still receiving calls from official-sounding people offering to help out because her computer "is being used for criminal activity." The difference now is that Janet's mother-in-law is wise to the scam.

The CEO of a regional bank told us that twice a year she brings in security consultants to "secret shop" her employees. She said, "I do it because it's important to test our vigilance about data security."

The security consultants use social engineering penetration techniques to see if they can get bank employees to give out customer information or bypass a security procedure. The techniques include things like posing as a bank employee or as an irate customer. The object of the tests is not to trick or punish the bank employees, but rather to probe for weak areas in security and then to strengthen the training and vigilance.

Are you too smart to be fooled?

At a presentation on identity theft awareness given by our local police department to a group of senior citizens, the instructor warned against giving personal information over the telephone. Everyone in the audience listened carefully, but one gentleman scoffed, "I'd never fall for that!"

Maybe he wouldn't fall for that particular trick, but no one is so smart that they can never be fooled. Professional identity thieves can be very convincing. Anyone can be fooled at least once.

Thieves are clever, quick, and often experienced. They catch you off guard by raising an alarm or by asking for help. Before you know it, you have fallen for one of their tricks.

Worse, embarrassment and humiliation cause many victims to hide the fact that they've been fooled.

What should you look out for?

There are four basic psychological techniques that social engineers will employ to get information and compliance from you:

Asking for assistance

With this technique, someone offers to help you, asks for your help, or apparently needs your help. As you engage in conversation and get involved, the identity thief will gather personal information from you without your realizing it. News stories tell of thieves posing as maintenance workers, utility workers, and Good Samaritans.

In Ocala, Florida, a man approached elderly women in a parking lot and "told them their cars appeared to be leaking fluid." The helpful man then asked the women to look for leaks while he sat in their cars and turned the steering wheel. Of course, the women later discovered that while they were distracted and looking for leaks, the man was stealing their wallets from their purses. [34]

In Northern Colorado, identity thieves posed as bank fraud investigators. They contacted bank customers and asked for their help in catching a dishonest teller. The victim follows the investigator's instructions, withdraws cash, and gives it to a bank "associate." By the time the victim realizes that the investigators were fakes, it is too late. [35]

Scam artists and identity thieves often pose as people who are trying to help you or who need your help. Always take time to report them to someone or check them out. Don't get distracted by their stories that are designed to play on your fears, sympathies, and desire to help.

Persuading you

With persuasion, someone attempts to win you over to comply with a request. Some persuasion techniques include flattery, name dropping, and appeals to emotion or logic.

A well-documented case of persuasive social engineering involves a young California man named

Cosmo. His story is told in the September 2012 issue of Wired Magazine. It shows how someone with a little information can easily get more.

Cosmo, at age 15, was a master social engineer and computer hacker. Before he was arrested, Cosmo succeeded in using the phone to talk his way past security and "into accounts on Amazon, Apple, AOL, PayPal, Best Buy, Buy.com, Live.com (think: Hotmail, Outlook, Xbox), and more."

Cosmo and his hacker friends specifically targeted high-level executives who supported the Stop Online Piracy Act (SOPA). The Wired article gives the details of how easy it was for Cosmo to gather bits of personal information and then breach individual accounts. To collect the personally identifiable information he needed, Cosmo searched online and, piecing things together, purchased Social Security numbers online, and persuaded customer service representatives and technicians to give him what he needed over the phone.

Cosmo's arrest and subsequent confession has helped companies do a better job of tightening their security and training employees to be careful about giving out information. [36]

However, it stands as a lesson to the many industries and businesses that are yet either unaware of the dangers or are careless. The window of opportunity for thieves and mischief-makers remains wide open.

Flattering and fawning on you

With this technique, someone intentionally makes himself or herself likable, and even charming, for the purpose of building a relationship they can then use to take advantage of you. This is calculated, ingratiating behavior.

The thief may be so kind and helpful that you feel obligated to give in return. Your defense against people who are always doing something for you is reminding yourself that you don't have to return their favors.

The identity thief may intentionally warm up to you, make himself or herself likable, and form a personal relationship in order to exploit it. Senior citizens are easy targets for this type of abuse because they are often lonely, may be somewhat isolated, or need help with the activities of daily living. The helpful new "friend" may turn out to be an identity thief.

A man on the Most Wanted list in Oregon "used his boyish charm to latch onto women. He then stole their credit cards, checks, cash, and high-ticket items before disappearing." [37]

One reported identity thief was a university professor in Seattle. The *Seattle Times* reports that the professor took students' Social Security numbers and used them to open checking accounts and to apply for credit cards. According to the news article, the professor applied for the cards but did not use them to make transactions. Nevertheless, he was opening the accounts. Who knew that a trusted university professor was an identity thief? He was described by co-workers as being "dynamic, articulate, and charismatic." [38]

Pay attention when someone who seems too good to be true enters your life. If other people you know begin to warn you that something doesn't seem right about a relationship, you should listen.

Intimidating you

A person may use authority or anger to bully you into giving them information. Intimidation may work because you will cooperate just to get rid of the angry person. [39]

How you respond to bullying or intimidation by someone posing as an official or irate customer makes you vulnerable to social engineering. According to security expert Paul Schumacher, "Many people do not have the strength of personality to stand up to bullying and to the threat of official action. Having clear and precise directives as to what to do when confronted by a challenge for access - with alternative actions if the first is not available . . . is mandatory for people to resist this, and many other, types of social engineering. It is the uncertainty that the social engineer exploits, together with the desire of people to be helpful to others." [40]

Don't be afraid to call for help or stall for time when a situation seems threatening. You don't have to give in to their demands. That angry authority figure or out of control customer could be a fake.

How should you change your behavior?

The behavior change necessary to combat social engineering is like the behavior training you receive in fire drills. In other words, your survival depends upon already having some plan of action in mind. You have to have some idea of what you will do or say when someone throws you off balance with a compliance tactic.

Social engineering is behavior-related. To combat the problem requires behavior change, continuing education, teamwork, and vigilance.

The bank we mentioned earlier in this chapter achieves behavior change by regularly training and testing the employees. You may not have access to that level of training, but you still can pick up a few techniques to improve how you protect your personal information.

Think about your behavior at your bank, your doctor's office, your phone company, or your city utilities office. What are you saying out loud that others can overhear?

A friend witnessed how easily people can be persuaded to speak information out loud as she sat in the waiting room of a walk-in medical clinic. A man walked up to the check-in desk and gave his name to the receptionist. She then began asking him questions from the patient registration form. Our friend heard all of the man's answers: his name, address, phone number, date of birth, and Medicare number.

How would you have responded if you had been the man checking in? Would you have requested a more private location before answering the questions?

Don't answer obediently for all to hear when a receptionist, sales person, or clerk asks for your personally identifiable information. Request to either fill out the form yourself or move the interview to a private location.

Having a prepared "refusal script" ready will help you break the habit of obedience to requests that put your information at risk. Convicted scam artist Tom Arnold recommends memorizing and practicing a few lines that you can say quickly and confidently. [41]

At the receptionist's window, or at any public location, when asked to state your personally identifiable information, say: "I don't say my information out loud in public. How can we do this privately?"

Clerks at retail checkout lanes are often required by their employer to ask for your phone number, mailing address, or email address. Have your refusal script ready. In most cases you are not required to provide the information and in all cases you do not have to answer the request for all to hear.

Having a little refusal script memorized is especially empowering when a salesman calls on the telephone. Tom Arnold recommends saying: "I'm sorry. This is not a good time. Thank you for calling." Then hang up immediately without listening to another word the salesman has to say.

How should you respond when you fall for a scam?

Even when professionals like bank and hospital employees are trained and have prevention plans in place, the best social engineers still can fool them.

When you discover that you've been taken in by a social engineering tactic, you'll feel angry and upset. You'll feel embarrassed and humiliated. Most people try to hide what has happened.

If the deception becomes public knowledge, the victim's feelings of humiliation and despair can become overwhelming. That's what happened to a London hospital nurse who was fooled by two radio disc jockeys impersonating Queen Elizabeth and Prince Charles on the telephone.

Believing that the DJs were the real Queen and Prince, the nurse put the call through to Duchess Kate Middleton's private nurse. The disc jockeys social-engineered their way into getting private information about Kate from the private nurse. The DJs then broadcast clips of the recording on the air.

Even though the call was a prank, the nurse who answered the phone could not endure the public embarrassment. Soon after the incident, she was found dead, a possible suicide. [42]

What's the lesson in this story?

The first lesson is to stop and think before complying with a request for information, especially over the phone. It's a good idea to stall for time. Tell the person that you need to either call them back or ask for permission before you can proceed. Listen to your intuition. If something doesn't feel right, then stop. The lesson is: stop and stall.

Never be afraid or embarrassed to check with someone else before you comply with requests for information, permission, or money.

A common social engineering trick goes like this. The phone rings during the night and you answer. The voice on the line says, "Grandma?" You say, "Johnny, is that you?"

"Johnny" then tells about getting into a jam and needing some quick cash. He tells you how to wire some money and asks you to "please, don't tell Mom and Dad."

Three individuals have told us, "My Grandma wired them $1,500 before she found out it wasn't me." The lesson is: trust but verify.

Social engineers succeed by persistence. Cut them off and don't let them wear you down. One older lady told us she tells sales people: "I have to run this by my son first." Come up with a line that works for you and stick with it.

The second lesson is that if you discover you've been scammed, deceived, or are a victim of fraud, don't be ashamed to tell your story. Don't be intimidated by proud people who think THEY are too smart ever to be fooled. "Pride ends in humiliation," says Proverbs, "while humility brings honor." [43] Sharing what happened to you when the bad guys closed in and the lessons you learned from the experience will help prevent someone else from becoming the next victim.

Recently we gave an identity theft awareness presentation to a local service organization. We began by asking: "Raise your hand if you've been a victim of identity theft." Not one hand went up. At the end of our talk during the question-and-answer session, several people shared personal stories about identity theft. What changed? The stories we shared made our audience feel safe about sharing their own experiences. Telling the stories changed our presentation from a lecture into a healing conversation.

Anyone can be tripped up by deception techniques. Ex-computer hacker Kevin Mitnick warns us that social engineers are artists who "toy with your trust, your desire to be helpful, your sympathy, and your human gullibility to get what they want."

"If you think you've never encountered one," said Mitnick, "you're probably wrong." [44]

Review

- You are not too smart to be fooled.

- Social engineering is the use of psychological techniques to gain your trust or to manipulate your behavior.

- Don't be ashamed to share your story if you are the victim of a trick, scam, or fraud. Your experience might help prevent someone else from becoming a victim.

- Share your story or safety tip about identity theft or social engineering by leaving a reply on our blog beatidentitytheftbook.com/blog.

Murphy's Laws

- Anything that can go wrong will go wrong.
- Nothing is as easy as it looks.
- Everything takes longer than you think.
- If everything seems to be going well, you have obviously overlooked something.
- Every solution breeds new problems.

Chapter 5

Costs and hidden costs of

identity theft

"It can cost you everything — your job, your lifestyle," said identity theft victim Darryl Greenridge.

For a period of 13 years, Greenridge struggled to regain control of his personally identifiable information that was being used by an identity thief.

It started when Greenridge went to renew his New York driver's license and discovered traffic violations on his record. The problem was, Greenridge had never had a traffic ticket. Over the next decade, the problem grew worse as the identity thief assumed Greenridge's total identity. He obtained a Texas driver's license, rented a house, got a cell phone, opened a bank account and took out loans, received a criminal record, and served jail time.

When the first clues surfaced, Greenridge had no way of knowing that his life would be forever changed by identity theft. Greenridge was afraid to change jobs. Background and credit checks would reveal a history that no employer would touch. He even had to take a DNA test to prove that he was not responsible for child support payments for the identity thief's child.

As the years went by, Greenridge suffered financially and became depressed. "I could have become suicidal," he said, "but in retrospect now I can smile about it a little bit." That smile is because, thanks to a determined Texas detective, Greenridge's identity thief finally was apprehended in Texas.

"Crimes such as this can be very detrimental to a person," said the detective who was instrumental in resolving the case. "It can take [the victims] as long or longer to rebuild their lives as it took for the thief to destroy it." [45]

The case of Darryl Greenridge is an extreme example of identity theft. It took years to track down the offender, and it will take years to overcome the damage.

How well do you understand your risk?

Regardless of whether your own experience with identity theft is extreme or minor, it's up to you to prevent theft, detect fraud, and prove your innocence. Most people underestimate their ability to do those three things.

On one level, that's a natural response. It's only after becoming a victim that you experience how much of your time, money, and even your opportunities identity theft can steal.

According to the FTC, between 2008 and 2012, the most reported categories of identity theft and fraud were:

- Miscellaneous Categories of Identity Theft (22%)

- Government Document and Government Benefit Fraud (19%)
- Credit Card Fraud (15%)
- Phone or Utilities Fraud (14%)
- Employment-related Fraud (11%)
- Bank Fraud (10%)
- Attempted Identity Theft (7%)
- Loan Fraud (4%)

The above categories give you an idea of where your risks are, but the FTC acknowledges that "many instances of identity theft or attempted identity theft are never reported." [46] This is especially true of medical identity theft, which falls into the "Miscellaneous Categories."

The FTC Consumer Sentinel Network website (ftc.gov/sentinel) publishes reports and fact sheets that reveal the top identity theft categories in your state each year.

Regardless of where you live, pay close attention to your Social Security record and credit card and utilities statements. Check your credit reports. The sooner you can detect identity theft and report it, the less time, money, and opportunities it will cost you.

The thief of your time

There are plenty of surveys and studies proclaiming the high costs of identity theft in terms of time spent restoring the damage. The cost estimates range from conservative to extreme.

One website claims: "The Federal Trade Commission (FTC) estimates . . . the average victims . . . devote 170 to 300 hours trying to recover his or her identity and to resolve theft-relates issues." [47] The author does not give a citation to back up this claim.

In a prepared statement, then (2005) Chairman of the FTC Deborah Platt Majoras stated: "The [FTC's] ID theft survey also found that victims of the two major categories of identity theft cumulatively spent almost 300 million hours – or an average of 30 hours per person – correcting their records and reclaiming their good names." [48]

According to surveys conducted each year by Javelin Research, the number of hours "spent resolving fraud has decreased steadily since 2004, reaching an all-time low of 12 hours in 2011 from 18 hours in 2004." [49]

How much time will identity theft cost you? Is it an average of 12 hours? 30 hours? Or 300 hours? The reality is that the costs of identity theft in terms of time are difficult, if not impossible, to measure. Nevertheless, everyone can agree that identify theft costs each victim something.

Counting the cost of identity theft cannot be limited to the minutes and hours spent on it. Twelve hours doesn't quantify the elevated stress, worry, and frustration you'll experience that carry over into the other hours of your life. Nor does it measure the impact your negative feelings will have on the lives of the people around you.

In addition, those 12 hours won't pass in one block of time, like working a 12-hour shift. You'll spend a few minutes here writing a letter or an hour there on hold and lots of time everywhere complaining to your family, friends, and coworkers.

Twelve hours doesn't include the time you'll spend waiting for a response from an agency. According to acting (2012) IRS Commissioner Steven Miller, the IRS "still had a backlog of 300,000 cases of people waiting for legitimate refunds after they were victims of fraud. It takes an average of six months to resolve a case." [50] Six months is a long time to wait if you are counting on using your income tax refund for something important.

Finally, an average resolution time of 12 hours doesn't take into account your opportunity cost, which is the lost opportunity to use those 12 hours in some productive way.

We've established that the burden of proof falls on you, the identity theft victim. Assuming that your situation is on the conservative end of the scale, wouldn't you agree that spending 12 hours to clear your name is a lot of time?

Now imagine that instead of taking 12 hours to resolve, your situation took up to 30 hours or 300 hours. In a statement read before a Senate Committee (2000), Maureen Mitchell said, "I have logged over 400 hours of time trying to clear our names and restore our good credit. Words are unable to adequately express the gamut of emotions that we have experienced as victims. The impact of being a victim of Identity Theft is all encompassing. It affects you physically, emotionally, psychologically, spiritually and financially. This has truly been a life altering experience." [51]

The thief of your financial well-being

The 2012 Javelin Research report also tells us that the average out-of-pocket cost per incident of identity fraud has dropped "to $354 in 2011 from $637 in 2004."

The fact that the time and cost per incident to resolve identity fraud have fallen from what they were in 2004 does not mean that identity theft is going away. It could mean any number of things, including that we are getting better at early detection, and that the thieves are getting harder to detect.

While most people use the terms "identity theft" and "identity fraud" interchangeably, Javelin Research distinguishes between the two. They limit the use of "identity theft" to instances when "someone's personal information" is taken and used without their permission, and reserve the term "identity fraud" for "the actual misuse of information for financial gain."

One reason why the costs of resolving an identity fraud incident are falling is that most banks, credit unions, and credit card companies will not hold the consumer accountable for the loss IF the loss is reported in a timely manner.

Generally, monetary losses from existing account fraud are less than losses from new account fraud because fraudulent activity in existing accounts is easier to detect. According to a report released by the California Public Interest Research Group, "in 2010, victims lost about $82 per person. Last year [2011], they

84

lost about $786 per person." The dramatic increase in lost money is attributed to the fact that victims may not become aware of new account fraud, and the activity may continue for a longer period of time. [52]

For example, by the time one 17-year-old Arizona girl discovered that she was a victim of new account fraud, the damage included "owing $600,000 in mortgage loans and another $100,000 in car loans and credit cards." Over a period of 15 years, identity thieves used the girl's Social Security number to acquire "at least three mortgages, refinancing twice, buying cars, and opening at least 42 credit card or charge accounts in her name." [53]

At the end of the day, most of the financial cost of identity theft to you will be in proving your innocence and in dealing with the after-effects.

The thief of your opportunities

In addition to the time and financial costs of identity theft, there are hidden, impossible-to-measure costs.

These include a spoiled reputation, damaged personal relationships, and lost opportunities.

We learned of a single mother who began receiving collection notices for medical bills that weren't hers. It turns out that a woman who was dying of cancer had checked into a hospital using the single mom's name, date of birth, and Social Security number.

The single mom was able to prove to the hospital that the charges were fraudulent and therefore was not required to pay the bills.

"But," she said, "it took me five years to get those collections off my credit report. And during that time, my children couldn't get student loans. My oldest had to drop out of college after the first semester. Neither one of them ever finished college. What could I do? What was the use of me going after someone who was dying?" she said. "An identity thief stole my children's future."

How can you get the help and support you need?

Before, during, and after an identity theft incident, you have a choice: you can either get help or go it alone.

Legal

As an identity theft victim, you must initiate the damage control. You must know and do what it takes to restore your records, credit, and reputation.

If your identity theft issue is difficult to resolve, it may be necessary to hire an attorney. Receiving good advice from the beginning is important because, in reality, every identity theft event is a legal event.

Most people don't discover how much attorneys can cost until they get into a legal situation. Attorneys cost a lot of money. For that reason, many people choose to go it alone, or they try turning to an attorney friend or family member.

This may surprise you, but one of the worst attorneys you can get is a friend or relative. One reason is because attorneys don't like getting involved in situations where they have an emotional stake in the outcome. It's the same reason why surgeons don't operate on family members.

Another reason why friends and relatives don't make good attorneys is because lawyers are all about billable hours. They need a specific number of billable hours to reach their income goals. Naturally then, an attorney's high-priority work is billable hours work. In fact, many attorneys work for firms that require them to meet production quotas in terms of billable hours.

When you expect your attorney friend or relative to help you for free in their spare time, or at a reduced rate, you are cutting into their billable hours time. Your "charity" case may not receive the amount of time and attention it deserves. This can cause resentment and damage the relationship you have with your friend or relative. Many people fail to understand the hidden, high cost of "free" or "cheap" until after the damage has been done.

Some people will never understand the hidden, high cost of "free" and will spend one dollar three times rather than spend two dollars once. When you need professional help to restore your identity, get the best you can afford. It's a bargain in the long run.

Emotional

No matter how small or how great the damage, the process of dealing with identity theft is stressful.

As an identity theft victim you can be "twice a victim" because companies, agencies, and individuals may not cooperate with your efforts to correct the record. You may be brushed aside or, worse, treated like a criminal.

The stress associated with identity theft is a greater concern than many people realize. Studies have demonstrated a clear link between high stress levels and health problems.

Stress-related health problems include: "anxiety, insomnia, muscle pain, high blood pressure, and a weakened immune system . . . stress can even contribute to the development of major illnesses, such as heart disease, depression, and obesity, or exacerbate existing illnesses." [54]

Imagine what might happen to your health if you add the stress of dealing with an identity theft incident on top of the stress you already experience from the events daily living.

Identity theft triggers the emotional process of loss and renewal. The process of adjusting to a loss is grief. When your loss is minimal, you may not notice any emotional response other than irritation at the inconvenience. However, when your loss is significant, you may experience deep emotional pain that requires time and support from others before there is healing.

In addition to the grief process, victims may struggle with feelings of embarrassment and humiliation. If you find yourself struggling emotionally, you may benefit from calling a local hotline, attending counseling, or joining a victim support group.

If you are a victim of crime, it is healthy to seek out counseling and spiritual healing. There's no benefit to yourself or to your family in allowing your spirit to feed on the anger, depression, and other negative emotions that rise to the surface when you experience loss. You can't change what happened, but you can control how you respond.

Learning to forgive can help you get your life back after an identity theft event. "The practice of forgiveness" says the Stanford Forgiveness Project, "has been shown to reduce anger, hurt, depression, and stress, and leads to greater feelings of hope, peace, compassion, and self confidence. Practicing forgiveness leads to healthy relationships as well as physical health. It also influences our attitude which opens the heart to kindness, beauty, and love." [55]

The Identity Theft Resource Center has some online resources for identity theft victims. Visit the ITRC website idtheftcenter.org/ or call the Center at 888-400-5530.

It's disheartening to look at all of the types of identity theft and to realize that in many instances, there is nothing you can do to prevent it from happening to you. Rather than fall victim to the dark night of the soul, get help.

Review

- Most people underestimate their ability to deter theft, detect fraud, and demonstrate their innocence.
- Identity theft steals your time, financial well-being, and opportunities.
- Victims of identity theft need help dealing with the crime, both legally and emotionally.

. . . many victims may not
understand their rights and
do not clearly understand
what steps they should take
to address identity theft . . .

An FTC Staff Report on a Survey of
Identity Theft Victims, page 5

March 2012

Chapter 6

How you can get help and support

You cannot ignore identity theft activity and hope it will go away on its own. You have to fight back. The fight is by nature a defensive game, since it's not possible for you to know in advance who the identity thieves are or when they will strike.

Should you buy an identity theft protection plan?

Consumer concern over identity theft has opened a growing market for identity theft protection products. There's some debate over whether the plans offer any real value, since there are some defensive actions you can take on your own.

You can always check your account balances online for free. One man told us that after identity thieves took money from his bank account, he now makes it a habit to check his bank account balance online every day.

You also can check your credit report for free online at annualcreditreport.com (or call them at 1-877-322-8228).

You can even ask the credit reporting companies to put a fraud alert or credit freeze on your account. The fraud alert must be renewed every 90 days, so you'll have to set a reminder. A fraud alert will require creditors to notify you if there is an attempt to open a credit account in your name.

So should you pay for an identity theft protection service? The magazine *Consumer Reports* is one of several publications that have published critical examinations of the identity theft protection service industry. The article "Debunking the hype over ID theft: You don't need a costly service to protect your good name"

(*Consumer Reports Money Adviser*. February 2012) cautions against paying for anything that you can do for yourself.

The *Consumer Reports* article points out that identity theft protection plans don't really solve the problem and, worse, may give consumers a false sense of security.

What is the value of early detection?

Finding ways to detect theft and fraud as soon as possible just makes common sense. Credit monitoring and other financial monitoring services are as necessary today as having smoke detectors, but they don't prevent identity theft any more than smoke detectors can prevent fires.

Monitoring services alert you that something is happening. However, they can miss something and give you a false sense of security. There's no substitute for your own vigilance.

The sooner you can discover that someone "has gotten in," the sooner you can stop the damage they can do to you. This is especially important for credit card and banking fraud because the financial institution may not have to reimburse your loss if you wait too long to report it.

It's true that credit monitoring is not fool-proof and that credit and banking issues account for only 1/5 of reported identity theft events. It's also true that many instances of identity theft, such as medical identity theft, are only discovered after the fact.

But the reality is that there are many, many people who don't have the skills or the time to do everything for themselves. Sometimes it's more efficient to pay an expert to do the job for you. What you decide about identity protection plans is a choice about living your life on your terms.

What's the least you should know before you enroll in a plan?

If you decide to buy a plan, then the question becomes: are these products living up to their claims?

The Consumer Federation of America's report "Best

Practices for Identity Theft Services: How Are Services Measuring Up?" can provide some clarity about what to look for in a service provider. [56] Among the many recommendations for identity theft protection services are that they should:

- not misrepresent their ability to protect consumers from identity theft;

- provide clear, accurate, and complete information about how they protect consumers and/or help them recover;

- be careful when referring to statistics in promoting their services;

- clearly disclose their cancellation and refund policies; and

- not misrepresent, directly or by implication, the benefits of insurance or guarantees that they offer.

What other things should you consider?

First, examine the claims the company makes about identity theft. Are the statistics about the crime realistic or inflated? This can be difficult to determine, depending upon whose numbers you see. At the very least, you should compare the advertised statistics with information on the FTC website ftc.gov. Be aware that statistics alone don't tell the whole story about identity theft.

While we are doing a better job of preventing some forms of identity theft, and financial institutions are willing (and in some cases legally required) to absorb the losses, the identity thieves are getting smarter and are always thinking of new areas.

Second, think about your own behavior. Studies have demonstrated that consumers have a "preference for insuring against probable small losses at the expense of the less probable but larger impact ones." [57] This means that people tend to overestimate the impact of a predictable event and underestimate the effect of a rare one. This is why people ask for details about how their health insurance plan will cover "preventive care," but make assumptions about how it will cover cancer treatment.

Third, most of the identity theft protection plans we've seen put a heavy emphasis on the front end of the problem, that is, the "prevention" or alert phase. Throughout this book we've told stories to illustrate how people's lives have been changed by an identity theft event. That's because what happens on the back end, after the damage has been done, is what will reshape your life.

With identity theft, it's in those less probable but larger impact events where you really need the most help. Look to see exactly how the plan will help you to restore your identity.

For tips on what to look for in an identity theft protection plan, go to beatidentitytheftbook.com. If you already own an identity theft protection plan and would like to tell others about how the service has been helpful, leave a reply to a blog post on beatidentitytheftbook.com/blog.

What's the difference between resolution and restoration?

An identity theft protection plan will generally make some promise of help in the event that you experience an identity theft incident. Exactly how they will help is often not clear, according to the "Best Practices for Identity Theft Services" report.

The report also outlines the services offered by several companies. One company says that "resolution services won't continue if the company concludes that that the problem will never be resolved." Another says "some identity theft service providers follow up with the entities that they contacted on behalf of their customers to ensure that the problems are resolved, while others do not."

Resolution services are the procedures for resolving a situation or dispute. These services can be as simple as providing a kit with instructions on how to restore your identity. Services might include counseling or assistance from a "resolution specialist."

In most cases, you will end up doing most of the work required to restore your identity, but hopefully any guidance or assistance you receive will end up saving you some time and money.

Restoration services are efforts made on your behalf to repair the damage. To receive these services, you will be required to sign a limited-power of attorney. This allows an investigator to do some of the work for you. A report issued by a credit union research and consulting firm explains that "the restoration companies also have the ability to restore the identity for the victim much faster because of the training and relationships they have with the credit reporting agency's [sic], DMV, Social Security Administration, and Post Office which all are contacted and notified that identity theft has taken place." [58]

The bottom line is that you need to read the fine print and ask questions about what's covered before you buy.

What protection plans do you already have in place?

You cannot stop identity theft from happening. We are of the opinion that it is better to have identity theft protection on multiple levels than it is to rely on a single solution. This includes having access to support or counseling that can help you deal with the emotional trauma that all crime victims experience.

Don't get hung up on areas where you may have some duplication of services. No single source can meet your every need in the face of an ever-changing crime.

The first step in protecting yourself, then, is to assess the options you already may have in place, or have available to you though your bank, credit card company, insurance company, or employer. These include:

- Identity theft protection plans
- Credit monitoring services
- Bank identity theft protection plans

- Credit card protection plans

- Homeowners insurance plans or endorsements

- Plans offered to you at work

After you find out what you have, then determine what's missing. Maybe you'll want to change your bank or credit card provider to a company that offers better protection. Maybe you'll decide to add a rider to your homeowner's insurance coverage or enroll in an identity theft protection plan.

What combination of solutions will give you peace of mind? Everyone is different, but Ockham's Razor says that the simplest solution is probably the right one. Look for identity theft protection plan benefits such as:

- Unlimited consultation before, during, and after an identity theft event

- Licensed investigators

- Clearly spelled out guarantees

- Clearly defined plan limitations

- Exactly what is monitored and how you will be notified

- How and when the alerts go out
- Hidden costs or fees

What about plans with legal services?

Some identity theft protection plans may provide you with legal representation in certain circumstances. A property, renters, or travel insurance policy may cover the cost of legal representation. Ask your agent or insurance company what your policy includes.

One thing to consider, however, is that insurance-provided legal help is going to look out for the best interest of the insurance company. Their best interest may not necessarily be your best interest.

One option is to purchase a separate legal protection plan. That way you'll have access to advice and services from attorneys that are looking out for you. You may also find that the service can help in other ways, since it won't be limited to incidents of identity theft or fraud.

For tips on what to look for in a legal protection plan, go to beatidentitytheftbook.com. If you already own a legal protection plan and would like to tell others about how the service has been helpful, leave a reply to a blog post on beatidentitytheftbook.com/blog.

What's the downside if you don't have an identity theft protection plan?

In spite of skepticism from its critics, the identity theft protection services industry continues to evolve and get better at what it does. An identity theft protection plan should be viewed as a strong complement to the other services and insurance protection you should have. It is not a single solution to the problem, but rather an important service that will work on your behalf to help resolve identity theft when it occurs.

When people first started using the internet, they were taken aback when viruses, spyware, and malware quickly showed up. After a while, it didn't take much persuasion to help people see the dangers of connecting a computer to the internet without first installing antivirus protection.

We're rapidly approaching the time when having multiple layers of identity theft protection is not an option. It is a necessity.

To determine the downside of not having an identity theft protection plan, ask yourself:

How might the crimes of identity theft and fraud change over the next five years?

Will they become less of a threat or will they grow worse?

What are the advantages of credit and other monitoring services, and do they outweigh the cost savings of monitoring everything on your own?

When you become a victim of identity theft, will you be better off with a restoration service to help you or can you go it alone?

What's the bottom line?

While no single source can cover all of the angles, more and more organizations, agencies, and services are stepping forward to address the crime of identity theft and help the victims.

At the end of the day as you look back, the value of the help you receive as an identity theft victim will not be so much about the up-front protection, the money you lose or save, the restoration process, or even bringing the criminal to justice. The value will be more about your emotional healing process, your integrity in coming to terms with what happened, and your ability to get on with your life.

Review

- You should check your account balances (at least monthly) and get your credit report on your own at annualcreditreport.com (at least annually).
- It can be efficient to hire experts to help you, even with things you could do for yourself.
- If you buy an identity theft protection plan, make sure it offers true restoration services.

We've all heard about it, again and again, but how many of us have actually taken the steps to protect our most valuable information and identities? In numbers that increase every day, identify theft is becoming an epidemic that threatens everyone.

"Steps You Should Take
in Preventing Identity Theft"

on FindLaw, a Thomson Reuters business

Chapter 7

Armed with a plan and prepared to fight

This book is a call for you to arm yourself with the knowledge, tools, and leverage that will make you effective in reducing your risk and fighting back against the modern crime wave, identity theft.

The very fact that it's necessary to issue a call to arms shows how dramatically criminal activity has changed our lives over the past two decades. To live worry free in today's world requires having access to a level of help that until now has been beyond reach for an average citizen.

The wealthy have lawyers and private investigators. They don't count the cost of getting help. Instead, they count the cost of doing without.

The not-wealthy have to count the cost of getting help, and likely chose to do without. That's why most people use the "emergency room" model to manage the risk of identity theft. They try to patch things up themselves, and only seek help when the situation is more than they can handle. Until a few, far-sighted companies saw the need and figured out a way to change the service delivery model, there was no alternative.

The alternative is a "preventive" or "wellness" model for obtaining legal help and identity theft restoration. The "preventive" model is available through legal protection plans and identity protection plans with restoration services.

The concept behind these plans is similar to how insurance products work. When many people pool their resources to share the risk, it significantly reduces the cost of delivering services when someone needs help.

Legal protection plans and identity theft plans are tools that help you reduce your risk. They are services that connect you with professionals who help you fight back when your rights have been violated. Unfortunately, many times the outcome of a situation does not depend on whether you are right or wrong, but whether you know how the law applies.

To answer the call to arms, you must reject procrastination, denial, and excuse-making. You must not wait for government or luck to favor you. The solution to the crime of identity theft starts with you. Do you really believe that?

You saw the risks of identity theft

After reading this book, you now have a better idea of what you reasonably can and can't do to prevent identity theft.

First, stop believing you can prevent identity theft from happening. We spoke with a law enforcement officer who told us about a training session he attended, taught by his regional director of Homeland Security. The director said, "Your personally identifiable information is out there in so many places that identity theft is just a numbers game. It's like your number is on a giant roulette wheel. Sooner or later, the ball will land on your number and it's going to be your turn."

Second, you can't always bring the offenders to justice even if you can find them. When the thief turns out to be a family member, victims are reluctant to go to the police. When the thief is a professional hacker operating from a foreign country, victims are unable to prosecute. Most identity thieves are never apprehended. A 2000 study estimates that an identity thief has less than a 1% chance of being caught. [59]

Third, you can't let down your guard. Identity thieves want to capture your personally identifiable information and then use it to commit or to cover up some kind of illegal activity. They never stop looking for opportunities.

Fourth, you must learn to guard against social engineering and to respond with appropriate non-compliance. This is one of the most important behavior changes you can make to protect your emotional and financial wellbeing.

Finally, you must not underestimate the scale of the damage control you might face. A minor incident of identity theft could set off a chain of worse events. When you become the victim of identity theft, it is up to you to initiate and manage the steps necessary to restore your accounts and records. Do you really want to have to go it alone?

You saw the need to put a plan in place

We've established the fact that much of your personally identifiable information is tucked away on countless databases, files, and archives. It is scattered across your lifetime. You don't know where all of it is; you can't prevent someone from stealing it.

The first thing you need when you are a victim of identity theft is help and support. The best way to get it is to prepare in advance of the need.

Forget the emergency room model. There is no 911 service, no ambulance, and no fire truck for identity theft. If you are to transform yourself from helpless victim to triumphant hero, then you'll have to embrace the solution.

Having an identity theft plan with restoration services, as well as a legal protection plan, is the best way to reduce your risk and fight back against identity theft.

Imagine the feeling of empowerment and peace of mind that comes from knowing in advance what your first phone call will be. Knowing that experts have your back goes a long way toward reducing the stress and emotional trauma that comes with being a crime victim.

An identity theft plan that includes restoration services puts licensed investigators on your case who can help you get through this in the most organized and efficient way possible. A legal protection plan puts attorneys on your side and gives you a resource that can help you make better decisions in every area of life.

Make it so

So let's don't wait until after the horse has been stolen to lock the barn door. "After becoming fraud victims," says the "2012 Identity Fraud Report," [60] "many victims say they are taking preventive measures against identity fraud." Do not wait until after your identity has been stolen to put a plan in place.

Don't complicate your decision to act. Protection plans are available for less than a dollar a day. At this level, your dilemma is less about who needs to be involved in the decision and more about who will be impacted the most if you procrastinate?

The cost of the solution is less than the cost of the problem. You'll save time, money, and stress if you'll take what you know now and turn it into action.

You are invited to take three steps now:

1. **Sign up.**

   1a. Enroll in a quality identity theft plan with restoration services BEFORE something happens.

   1b. Enroll in a legal protection plan.

2. **Check up.**

   2a. Look at your credit report regularly by using annualcreditreport.com.

   2b. Trust but verify. When someone asks you for information or wants access to an area where information is kept, take time to verify that they are legitimate.

3. **Speak up.**

   3a. Start talking about identity theft with other people. Share stories. Raise awareness.

   3b. Protect your privacy. Don't comply with requests for your information when others can overhear you or when you think the request is unjustified.

Paint a picture of a better possibility.

Imagine yourself armed with a plan and resources to fight back against identity theft. You feel good about yourself because you have reduced the risks that come from a crime you can't prevent.

Imagine yourself with knowledge, tools, and leverage that help you maintain your ability to lead a normal life in a society where your rights are protected under the rule of law.

Imagine feeling good about your future because you have taken smart steps to protect:

- *Your reputation in your community,* which allows you to work in your chosen field;
- *Your credit,* which allows you to buy property (a home, car, etc.), borrow money (for a home or student loans), and to save for the future (retirement, goals, and emergencies);

- *Your personal records* (Social Security, driver's license, medical, etc.), which allow you to conduct business and transactions with integrity, safety, and security; and

- *Your family,* which includes your children and their future and your rights to settle an estate and receive, or leave, an inheritance.

Imagine knowing that the very minute you discover yourself a victim of identity theft, you know exactly who to call and where to go for help.

Imagine . . . this could be you.

120

Resources

Four immediate steps to take if you suspect or know that your identity has been stolen

Depending on the situation, there are immediate steps you should take if you suspect that your identity has been stolen or your accounts have been compromised.

First: Immediately call every financial institution involved. This could be your bank, credit card companies, online payment service, or utility providers. Write down the names of the persons you speak with and keep detailed notes of your conversations.

Second: Contact one of the three credit reporting companies to place a fraud alert on your credit line and order a free credit report. It doesn't cost anything to place a fraud alert, and it's good for 90 days.

Equifax 1-800-525-6285

Experian 1-888-397-3742

TransUnion 1-800-680-7289

Placing a credit freeze on your credit file prevents businesses, lenders, or employers from reviewing your credit report. There may be a cost to freeze and un-freeze your file or time limits to the freeze, depending on your state laws.

Regardless of the situation, it may be a good idea to report your identity theft incident to your state Attorney General's office. Find your state Attorney General's office on the National Association of Attorneys General website naag.org/current-attorneys-general.php.

Third: Call your local law enforcement and file a police report. Make sure you receive a copy of the police report; you may need it later.

Fourth: You may also file an identity theft complaint with the FTC online at ftc.gov/complaint, or by calling the FTC at 1-877-438-4338. Your complaint will be added to the national database and will help law enforcement in their investigations.

The FTC has many resources and tips on the following website: ftc.gov/idtheft.

You can order the FTC's helpful publications, such as the workbook "Taking Charge: What To Do If Your Identity is Stolen."

Consumer advocacy groups

There are many independent advocacy groups that offer resources and advice on identity theft. This list of resources is not a complete list. Inclusion on this list does not necessarily mean that we are endorsing everything about the company, organization, or service.

Websites may change and new or better resources may become available. Go to the resources page on beatidentitytheftbook.com to see our updated list.

As you search online, be wary of a website that tries to sell you something or requires you to give your email address or other contact information before you can see the solutions. Also, beware of impostor websites. Double check your spelling and make sure you are on a legitimate website.

This list will help you get started.

Annual Credit Report: annualcreditreport.com or call 1-877-322-8228

Anti-Phishing Working Group: antiphishing.org

Consumer Federation of America: IDtheftinfo.org

ConsumersUnion: defendyourdollars.org

Cyber Street Smart: cyberstreetsmart.org

Identity Theft Resource Center: idtheftcenter.org

Internal Revenue Service: irs.gov/identitytheft or call 1-800-908-4490

Medical Information Bureau: mib.com or call 1-866-692-6901 (request your MIB consumer file, if one exists)

OnGuardOnline: onguardonline.gov

Opt Out of Prescreened Offers for Credit and

    Insurance: optoutprescreen.com or call 1-888-567-

    8688. The phone number and website are operated

    by the major consumer reporting companies.

Privacy Rights Clearinghouse: privacyrights.org

A word about passwords and PIN numbers

Strong passwords are a combination of upper and lower case letters, numbers, and symbols. The longer the password is, the longer it will take to crack.

To make your passwords easier to remember, try coming up with a phrase that you can convert into a password. For example: "Lions, tigers, and bears, oh my!" becomes the nine character password LtbOm!81$.

Computer hackers and identity thieves do not sit at a keyboard and guess passwords. They crack passwords by running sophisticated password-cracking software that can evaluate your password at speeds of one hundred billion guesses per second. [61]

Passwords of nine characters or more are harder to crack than are passwords of eight characters or less. Always include a capital letter and a symbol in your password.

Is your password on this list?

Top ten most commonly used passwords: [62]

1. Password1
2. welcome
3. password
4. Welcome1
5. welcome1
6. Password2
7. 123456
8. Password01
10. Password3

Top ten most hacked passwords: [63]

1. 123456
2. password
3. welcome
4. ninja
5. abc123
6. 123456789
7. 12345678

8. sunshine
9. princess
10. qwerty

Are you surprised by some of the most commonly used or hacked passwords? How strong is your most commonly used password?

PIN numbers

PIN numbers are four-digit numerical passwords that are used to protect your financial accounts. Your PIN number is required for transactions at an ATM or point of sale.

To make your PIN number more secure, never use consecutive numbers such as 1234, or consecutive key pad numbers such as 8520 (numbers in a vertical column on the key pad). Don't use combinations of numbers that are related to something that could be known about you, such as your birthday or house number.

Don't write your PIN number down on anything you carry with you in your purse, wallet, or date book. If you must write down a PIN number in order to remember it, try to conceal the number by writing it down as a phone number in your list of contacts. For example, you could create a contact entry for "Billy Smith 555-555-5555". Billy's area code and 3-digit exchange number would be correct for your area, but the last four digits would be the PIN number you want to conceal.

Even better, you could create two contacts. The first contact's "phone number" would contain the first two digits of your PIN number, and the second contact's "phone number" would contain the last two digits.

A word about paper shredders

Buy a good cross-cut shredder. Use it for everything, including receipts and junk mail. Shred everything.

If you have a lot of paper to shred, look for a local shredder service. Generally you have two options. Either you can take your papers to the shredder location, or the service will drive a mobile shredder unit to your location.

There are two things to look for in a shredder service. First, look for a service that is certified by an organization such as the National Association for Information Destruction (NAID). You can search for an NAID certified provider at naidonline.org. Second, look for a service that will shred your paper while you watch on location. Avoid doing business with a mobile shredder service that picks up your paper and trucks it to another location for shredding.

List of ways your identity can be stolen:

- Criminal violations in your name
- Tax fraud
- Debt collections
- Driver's license
- Investment fraud
- Mail theft
- Use of your address

- Property transfers
- Medical identity theft
- Insurance fraud
- Passport fraud
- Phone fraud
- Social Security numbers
- Student loans
- Student records database [64]
- Synthetic identity theft (combining information from more than one person to create a "synthetic" identity)
- Use of a child's identity
- Obtaining employment
- Loan and payday loan fraud
- Opening a new account under your name
- Existing account takeover fraud
- *The list can go on as far as the criminal mind can imagine . . .*

About the authors

Isabel Hogue

Isabel is a licensed insurance agent in Indiana, specializing in health and life products.

J.R. Woodrum

J.R. sold real estate in Indiana for 11 years. He has a background in not-for-profit management, radio, and consumer sales.

Both Isabel and J.R. are LegalShield independent associates. They offer legal and identity theft protection plans to individuals and employee groups.

Isabel and J.R. host the sales training program *WeeklySalesBuilder.com.*

An invitation from the authors

Many of our readers are eager to take action and get started as soon as possible with an identity theft protection plan with restoration services and possibly a legal protection plan.

The person who gave you this book may be able to help you.

We've assisted many people in following the steps we recommend. We would love to do the same for you.

We invite you to schedule a confidential consultation over the phone. To schedule a consultation, call 765-323-8347.

To take a confidential, online risk assessment, go to beatidentitytheftbook.com. You'll learn where your biggest risks are and what you can do to reduce them.

We hope you'll accept our invitation to visit beatidentitytheftbook.com/blog. Reply to a blog post and share your own story or tell other readers about the most important thing you learned from this book.

You can also write a review on Amazon.com

.

How to contact us

Email
help@beatidentitytheftbook.com

Phone
765-323-8347

Website and blog
beatidentitytheftbook.com

Facebook
Search for Beat-Identity-Theft-Book and give us a Like

Amazon.com and Createspace.com
Please write a review on Amazon.com.

Quantity discounts are available.

Send your request to help@beatidentitytheftbook.com
or call 765-323-8347

Acknowledgments

We are grateful to

- The many people who shared their identity theft experiences with us,
- Karen Hatke, our editor, for making this a better book,
- Our Thursday afternoon study group, and
- Jerry and Sharon, our spouses.

138

Notes

[1] PRWEB. "Identity theft protection services in the US industry market research report now available from IBISWorld." November 12, 2012. http://www.prweb.com/releases/2012/11/prweb10118354.htm. Accessed 5Mar2013.

[2] Quirk, Mary Beth. "Identity theft suspect has the misfortune to run into his victim at the bank" consumerist.com, July 17, 2012. http://consumerist.com/2012/07/17/identity-theft-suspect-has-the-misfortune-to-run-into-his-victim-at-the-bank/. Accessed 19Feb2013.

[3] This story was told to us by a woman in Tipton, Indiana. February 6, 2013.

[4] Paraphrased from Prepared Statement of the Federal Trade Commission on Identity Theft, by Betsy Broder, speaking before the Committee on Banking and Financial Services, United States House of Representatives, Washington, D.C., September 13, 2000. http://www.ftc.gov/os/2000/09/idthefttest.htm. Accessed 1 Jan 2013.

[5] Hoffman, Sandra K. and Tracy G. McGinley. *Identity Theft: A Reference Handbook* (Contemporary World Issues). ABC-CLIO, LLC. (2010). According to Hoffman and McGinley (p. 27), "the majority (60%) of identity theft cases involved a network" and "a network is defined as two or more individuals working together to perpetrate a crime."

[6] Hathaway, Melissa. "Ten thousand identity theft rings operating in the United States." Identity Theft Resource Center Blog, December 20, 2012. http://www.idtheftcenter.org/artman2/publish/Blog_FinancialID T/Ten-Thousand-Identity-Theft-Rings-Operating-in-the-United-States.shtml. Accessed 13July2013.

[7] Federal Trade Commission. "Consumer Sentinel Network Data Book, January - December 2012." Released February 2013. http://www.ftc.gov/sentinel/reports/sentinel-annual-reports/sentinel-cy2012.pdf. Accessed 13July2013.

[8] Symantec. "Data breaches that could lead to identity theft." Symantec.com. No date. http://www.symantec.com/threatreport/topic.jsp?id=threat_activi ty_trends&aid=data_breaches_that_could_lead. Accessed 13July2013. See the Norton CyberCrime Index http://us.norton.com/?cci=on&s_tnt=22618:0:0. Accessed 13July2013.

[9] South Carolina Department of Revenue - Security Breach Information. http://www.sctax.org/security.htm. Accessed 5Mar2013.

[10] Barr, Jody. "First SC hacking victims come forward." WISTV.com. November 19, 2012. http://www.wistv.com/story/20140487/first-sc-hacking-victims-come-forward. Accessed 13July2013.

[11] Open Security Foundation. "Data loss statistics." No date. http://datalossdb.org/statistics. Accessed 13July2013.

[12] Sutherly, Ben. "Hospitals use patient data to target ads." Columbus Dispatch, November 12, 2012. http://www.dispatch.com/content/stories/local/2012/11/12/hos pitals-use-patient-data-to-target-ads.html. Accessed 05May2013.

[13] Simon, Stephanie. "Student database backed by Gates Foundation jazzes tech startups, spooks parents." Reuters, March 3, 2013. "Local education officials retain legal control over their students' information. But federal law allows them to share files in their portion of the database with private companies selling educational products and services."

http://www.huffingtonpost.com/2013/03/03/student-database-gates-foundation_n_2800684.html. Accessed 27Apr2013.

[14] Pullman, Joy. "Education Dept. helps leak students' personal data." The Washington Examiner (Opinion), March 21, 2013. "The more people and organizations have access, and the bigger a treasure trove these databases become, the more likely security breaches become." http://washingtonexaminer.com/education-dept.-helps-leak-students-personal-data/article/2525112. Accessed 27Apr2013.

[15] Silvestrini, Elaine. "Loose data aids identity thieves." The Tampa Tribune, May 5, 2013. http://tbo.com/health/medical-news/loose-data-aids-identity-thieves-b82483075z1. Accessed 05May2013.

[16] Privacy Rights Clearinghouse. "Schoenbar Middle School, Ketchikan, Alaska." Chronology of Data Breaches. Information Source: California Attorney General. May 3, 2013. http://www.privacyrights.org/data-breach/new. Accessed 13July2013.

[17] Voravong, Sophia. "Former Purdue student sentenced for ID theft, fraud." Lafayette Journal and Courier, January 8, 2011. http://www.tippecanoe.in.gov/egov/docs/1293743584_54992.pdf. Accessed 5Jan 2013.

[18] sfgate.com. "Ore. authorities: ID theft ring hit 800 mailboxes." sfgate.com. May 15, 2013. http://www.sfgate.com/news/crime/article/Ore-authorities-ID-theft-right-hit-800-mailboxes-4518331.php. Accessed 15May2013.

[19] Robertson, Jordan. "Top credit agencies say hackers stole celebrity reports." Bloomberg Businessweek (March 12, 2013). http://www.businessweek.com/news/2013-03-12/equifax-transunion-say-hackers-stole-celebrity-reports. Accessed 13Mar2013.

[20] Horstman, Barry M. "Heat steps up in voter fraud investigation: Hamilton County officials plan 28 subpoenas as criminal charges loom." news.cincinnati.com. February 5, 2013. http://news.cincinnati.com/article/20130205/NEWS/302050144

/EXCLUSIVE-Heat-steps-up-voter-fraud-investigation. Accessed 12May2013.

21 Javelin Strategy & Research. 2012 Identity Fraud Report: Partnering with Law Enforcement (February 2012). https://www.javelinstrategy.com. Accessed 5Feb 2013.

22 Charette, Robert. "Smartphones becoming gateways to identity theft." IEEE Spectrum. February 24, 2012. http://spectrum.ieee.org/riskfactor/telecom/wireless/smartphones-becoming-gateways-to-identity-theft. Accessed 13July2013.

23 Taleb, Nassim Nicholas. *The Black Swan: The Impact of the Highly Improbable* (2008)

24 Sigsworth, Marc. "I was falsely branded a paedophile." BBC news magazine, 3 April 2008. http://news.bbc.co.uk/2/hi/uk_news/magazine/7326736.stm. Accessed 19Feb2013.

25 Federal Trade Commission. Consumer Sentinel Network Data Book for January - December 2012 (March 2011) http://www.ftc.gov/sentinel/reports/sentinel-annual-reports/sentinel-cy2010.pdf. Accessed 5 Jan 2013.

26 Isikoff, Michael. "Bernanke victimized by identity fraud ring." thedailybeast.com, Aug 24, 2009. http://www.thedailybeast.com/newsweek/2009/08/24/bernanke-victimized-by-identity-fraud-ring.html. Accessed 19Feb2013.

27 This story was told to us in 2012 by Good Mary. We've changed her name to protect her identity.

28 ITRC Solution 5 – Ordering a Child's Credit Report. Identity Theft Resource Center. http://www.idtheftcenter.org/artman2/publish/v_art_solutions/Solution_5.shtml. Accessed 26Apr2013.

29 Dolan, Pamela Lewis. "Medical ID theft: double danger for doctors." amednews, Aug. 6, 2012. http://www.ama-assn.org/amednews/2012/08/06/bisa0806.htm. Accessed 5Jan2013.

30 Gregg, Michael. "Why your medical records are no longer safe." Huffington Post. January 17, 2013.

http://www.huffingtonpost.com/michael-gregg/privacy-medical-records_b_2473458.html. Accessed 13July2013.

31 Broward, Charles. "More arrests in scheme involving identity theft from Shands hospitals." Jacksonville.com. April 23, 2013. http://jacksonville.com/news/crime/2013-04-23/story/more-arrests-scheme-involving-identity-theft-shands-hospitals?utm_source=feedburner&utm_medium=feed&utm_campaign=Feed%3A+JacksonvillecomMostPopularStories+(Jacksonville.com%3A+Most+Popular+Stories)#ixzz2RcaCTUnz. Accessed 26Apr2013.

32 Adams, David. "Florida hit by 'tsunami' of tax identity fraud." Reuters, February 17, 2013. http://www.reuters.com/article/2013/02/17/us-usa-tax-fraud-idUSBRE91G05M20130217. Accessed 17Feb2013.

33 Levin, Adam. "Consumer Reports got it dangerously wrong on identity theft." The Huffington Post, March 19, 2013. Levin referred to a "national poll last month which found that nearly 40 percent of Americans believe 'identity theft is not a serious problem.'" http://www.huffingtonpost.com/adam-levin/consumer-reports-got-it-d_b_2904286.html. Accessed 27Apr2013.

34 Ocala Star-Banner. "Deputies: seniors beware of thief posing as helper." Ocala Star-Banner, August 23, 2007. http://news.google.com/newspapers?id=lgVQAAAAIBAJ&sjid=cwkEAAAAIBAJ&pg=1087%2C3769587. Accessed 16May2013.

35 Tiller, Cris. "New fraud scheme hits Northern Colorado: fraudsters pose as internal security investigators." Loveland Reporter-Herald & reporterherald..com. May 6, 2013. http://www.reporterherald.com/news/larimer-county/ci_23184293/new-fraud-scheme-hits-northern-colorado. Accessed 16May2013.

36 Honan, Mat. "Cosmo, the hacker 'god' who fell to earth." Wired Magazine, September 11, 2012. http://www.wired.com/gadgetlab/2012/09/cosmo-the-god-who-fell-to-earth/all/. Accessed 31Dec2012.

[37] Bella, Rick. "'Most wanted' Clackamas County fugitive arrested in Mexico." OregonLive.com, September 15, 2010. http://www.oregonlive.com/clackamascounty/index.ssf/2010/09/most_wanted_clackamas_county_f.html. Accessed 27Apr2013.

[38] Carter, Mike. "Professor sentenced in fraud." Seattle Times Company, 2000. http://community.seattletimes.nwsource.com/archive/?date=20000817&slug=4037440. Accessed 5 Jan 2013.

[39] Microsoft TechNet Security Tech Center. "How to protect insiders from social engineering threats." August 18, 2006. http://technet.microsoft.com/en-us/library/cc875841.aspx#XSLTsection123121120120. Accessed 22Feb2013.

[40] Kabay, M.E. "Social engineering in penetration testing: intimidation." Security Strategies Alert, November 8, 2007. http://www.networkworld.com/newsletters/2007/1105sec2.html. Accessed 22Feb2013.

[41] Stark, Lisa. "Outsmarting the con artists: top 5 ways to avoid scams." ABC News. March 26, 20012. http://abcnews.go.com/Business/outsmarting-scam-artists-tips-avoid-advantage/story?id=15990100. Accessed 08Sep2013.

[42] CBS/AP. "Nurse in Duchess Kate hoax dead in apparent suicide." December 7, 2012. http://www.cbsnews.com/8301-207_162-57557775/nurse-in-duchess-kate-hoax-dead-in-apparent-suicide/. Accessed 22Feb2013.

[43] Proverbs 29:23. *The Holy Bible*, New Living Translation, copyright 1996, 2004, 2007. Tyndale House Publishers, Inc. Carol Stream, IL 60188.

[44] Mitnick, Kevin and William L. Simon. *The Art of Deception: Controlling the Human Element of Security*. http://fr.thehackademy.net/madchat/esprit/textes/The_Art_of_Deception.pdf. Accessed 6Feb2013.

[45] Johnston, Alyssa. "Man charged with identity theft: New Yorker fought 13 years to clear name." Times Record News, Wichita Falls, Texas.

http://www.timesrecordnews.com/news/2013/may/04/man-charged-with-identity-theft/. Accessed 1Jun2013.

[46] Federal Trade Commission, Consumer Sentinel Network Data Book for January - December 2012 (March 2011). http://www.ftc.gov/sentinel/reports/sentinel-annual-reports/sentinel-cy2010.pdf. Accessed 5Jan2013.

[47] hassassociates. "What's new in identity theft protection?" hassassociaties-online.com. March 14, 2013. http://hassassociates-online.com/articles/2013/03/14/whats-new-in-identity-theft-protection/. Accessed 13July2013.

[48] Majoras, Deborah Platt. "Prepared statement of the Federal Trade Commission before the Committee on Commerce, Science, and Transportation U.S. Senate on data breaches and identity theft." Federal Trade Commission. June 16, 2005. http://www.ftc.gov/os/2005/06/050616databreaches.pdf. Accessed 13July2013.

[49] Javelin Strategy & Research. 2012 Identity Fraud Report: Partnering with Law Enforcement (February 2012). https://www.javelinstrategy.com. Accessed 5Feb2013.

[50] Adams, David. "Florida hit by 'tsunami' of tax identity fraud." Reuters, February 17, 2013. http://www.reuters.com/article/2013/02/17/us-usa-tax-fraud-idUSBRE91G05M20130217. Accessed 17Feb2013.

[51] Mitchell, Maureen. "Statement of Maureen Mitchell, Senate subcommittee hearing technology terrorism March 7, 2000" ftc.gov. September 21, 2000. http://www.ftc.gov/bcp/workshops/idtheft/comments/mitchell maureen.htm. Accessed 13July2013.

[52] Anand, Anika. "Financial loss from identity theft increasing, report says." Californiawatch.org, June 28, 2012. http://californiawatch.org/dailyreport/financial-loss-identity-theft-increasing-report-says-16845. Accessed 04May2013.

[53] Brenoff, Ann. "Teenager owes $600,000 in mortgage loans after ID theft." October 14, 2011.

http://realestate.aol.com/blog/2011/10/14/teenager-owes-600-000-in-mortgage-loans-after-id-theft/. Accessed 04May2013.

54 Sifferlin, Alexandra, "The most stressed-out generation? Young adults." Time, Feb. 07, 2013. http://healthland.time.com/2013/02/07/the-most-stressed-out-generation-young-adults/. Accessed 15Mar2013.

55 The Stanford Forgiveness Project. 9 Steps. http://learningtoforgive.com/9-steps/. Accessed 22Feb2013.

56 Consumer Federation of America. "Best practices for identity theft services: how are they measuring up?" Consumer Federation of America, April 18, 2012. http://www.consumerfed.org/pdfs/Studies.BestPracticesMeasuringUpReport.4.17.12.pdf. Accessed 22Feb2013.

57 Taleb, Nassim Nicholas. *The Black Swan: The Impact of the Highly Improbable* (2008)

58 Callahan & Associates (a credit union research and consulting firm). CreditUnions.com. "Identity restoration vs. identity resolution." April 9, 2004. http://www.creditunions.com/articles/identity-restoration-vs-identity-resolution/. Accessed 5Feb2013.

59 Bourne, Mary Lou G., and Michael L. Deaton. "The dynamics of identity theft: a comparison of symptomatic and systemic solutions." James Madison University, 2005. http://www.systemdynamics.org/conferences/2005/proceed/papers/BOURN189.pdf. Accessed 13July2013.

60 Javelin Strategy & Research. "2012 identity fraud report: partnering with law enforcement." javelinstrategy.com. February 2012. Page 22.

61 Ponio, John. "The difference a symbol makes." June 8, 2012. http://insanetek.com/news/1-web-and-industry-news/1199-the-difference-a-symbol-makes. Accessed 09Sep2013.

62 Nguyen, Tuan C. "Top 10 most 'hacked' passwords: '123456,' 'ninja'". CBS Interactive Inc., July 16, 2012. http://www.smartplanet.com/blog/thinking-tech/top-10-most-

8216hacked-passwords-8216123456-8216ninja/12315. Accessed
8Feb2013.

⁶³ Ibid.

⁶⁴ "Simon, Stephanie. "Student Database Backed By Gates
Foundation Jazzes Tech Startups, Spooks Parents." Reuters, March
3, 2013. "Local education officials retain legal control over their
students' information. But federal law allows them to share files in
their portion of the database with private companies selling
educational products and services."
http://www.huffingtonpost.com/2013/03/03/student-database-
gates-foundation_n_2800684.html. Accessed 27Apr2013.

Pullman, Joy. "Education Dept. helps leak students' personal
data." The Washington Examiner (Opinion), March 21, 2013.
"The more people and organizations have access, and the bigger a
treasure trove these databases become, the more likely security
breaches become." http://washingtonexaminer.com/education-
dept.-helps-leak-students-personal-data/article/2525112. Accessed
27Apr2013.

Your student records, or your child's records, are being
consolidated into massive databases that can be accessed by
researchers, government agencies, and marketers. Any database is
vulnerable to a data breach.